D1442826

HIP-HOP
DANCE

By Audrey DeAngelis and Gina DeAngelis

CONTENT CONSULTANT

RACHEL RAIMIST, PHD
ASSOCIATE PROFESSOR
DEPARTMENT OF JOURNALISM & CREATIVE MEDIA
UNIVERSITY OF ALABAMA

Essential Library

An Imprint of Abdo Publishing | abdopublishing.com

Published by Abdo Publishing, a division of ABDO, PO Box 398166, Minneapolis, Minnesota 55439. Copyright © 2018 by Abdo Consulting Group, Inc. International copyrights reserved in all countries. No part of this book may be reproduced in any form without written permission from the publisher. Essential Library™ is a trademark and logo of Abdo Publishing.

Printed in the United States of America, North Mankato, Minnesota
042017
092017

**THIS BOOK CONTAINS
RECYCLED MATERIALS**

Cover Photo: Shutterstock Images
Interior Photos: Evan Agostini/Invision/AP Images, 5, 8, 13; E. Q. Roy/Shutterstock Images, 6; Olivier Douliery/Sipa USA/AP Images, 10; John D. Kisch/Separate Cinema Archive/Moviepix/Getty Images, 15; Library of Congress, 19; 7 Continents History/Everett Collection, 17; Everett Collection/Newscom, 23, 24–25; Terrence Jennings/Polaris/Newscom, 27; Linda Vartoogian/Archive Images/Getty Images, 29; Leslie McGhie/WireImage/Getty Images, 31; ZUMA Press Inc/Alamy, 33; Michael Ochs Archives/Getty Images, 36–37; Shutterstock Images, 39, 47, 90; Pymca/Universal Images Group/Newscom, 41; iStockphoto, 42–43; Mario Cabrera/AP Images, 49; Linda Vartoogian/Archive Photos/Getty Images, 52–53; Sthanlee B. Mirador/Pacific Rim/Newscom, 56–57; Sydney Brink/Sedalia Democrat/AP Images, 59; Kyodo/Newscom, 62–63; Craig F. Walker/Boston Globe/Getty Images, 65; Kevin Terrell/AP Images, 67; Crash imageSpace/Splash News/Newscom, 68–69; Pictorial Press/Alamy, 71; Sam Emerson/Summit Entertainment/Everett Collection, 74–75; Frank Micelotta Archive/Hulton Archive/Getty Images, 76–77; The Age/Fairfax Media/Getty Images, 79; Rob Vickery/Barcroft Media/Getty Images, 81; Evan Agostini/AP Images, 83; Frank Micelotta/Invision/AP Images, 85; Dan Steinberg/Invision/Huading Film Awards/AP Images, 86–87; David Cheskin/AP Images, 92–93; Rainer Jensen/picture-alliance/dpa/AP Images, 95; Isaac Brekken/AP Images, 96–97

Editor: Heidi Schoof
Series Designer: Jake Nordby

Publisher's Cataloging-in-Publication Data
Names: DeAngelis, Audrey ; DeAngelis, Gina, authors.
Title: Hip-hop dance / by Audrey and Gina DeAngelis.
Description: Minneapolis, MN : Abdo Publishing, 2018. | Series: Hip-hop insider |
    Includes bibliographical references and index.
Identifiers: LCCN 2016962250 | ISBN 9781532110283 (lib. bdg.) |
    ISBN 9781680788136 (ebook)
Subjects: LCSH: Hip-hop--Juvenile literature. | Hip-hop dance--Juvenile literature.
Classification: DDC 793.3--dc23
LC record available at http://lccn.loc.gov/2016962250

CONTENTS

1 HIP-HOP MAKES
HISTORY

Twelve figures in clothing reminiscent of the 1700s whirl across a stage, surrounded by brick and beams that suggest the rough-and-tumble, long-ago port of New York City. For more than an hour, these dancers have controlled time, racing through decades of history and slowing bullets to a snail's pace. And they won't stop for nearly two more hours. They are passengers in New York Harbor, soldiers in a ragtag army. They cheer the main character as he disses his enemies and, minutes later, laugh at his failures. Their constant motion crosses boundaries. At various moments, they break, krump, pop, waltz, and do a thousand other things, all in the service of telling a story through movement.

Lin-Manuel Miranda, *center*, was the first actor to play the role of Alexander

Hamilton opened on Broadway on August 6, 2015, at the historic Richard Rodgers Theatre in Times Square.

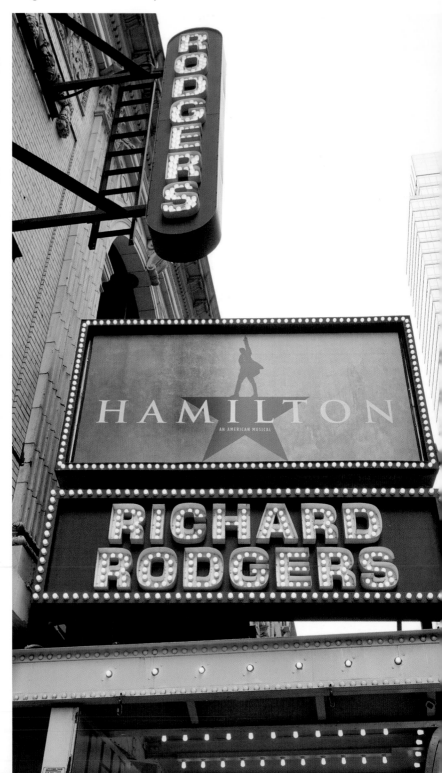

According to Lin-Manuel Miranda, the writer of the musical and original lead actor, Alexander Hamilton's life story embodies hip-hop. It is only natural, then, that Miranda used the words, attitude, culture, practitioners, and dance of hip-hop to tell the story of the first US treasury secretary. Second only to the rapid-fire record number of words for any musical, dance is the engine that drives this high-energy show to its many climaxes, tearful lows, and fateful conclusion.

Performances of *Hamilton* had been sold out since its off-Broadway opening at the Public Theater in January 2015. Still in 2017, the show was sold out months in

HIP-HOP AND . . . HAMILTON?

Alexander Hamilton grew up in a low-income, single-parent household in the Caribbean. When he was 10 or 12, he and his mother contracted the same severe illness, and his mother died. Orphaned, he got a job as a clerk for a trading company. As a teenager, he wrote an account of a hurricane that won attention and donations from residents of the West Indies to send him to school in North America. He landed in New York. From there, he eventually became General George Washington's right-hand man during the American Revolution (1775–1783). Afterward, he helped ratify the US Constitution and found the US Treasury, all largely on the strength of his own writing and brainpower. As Miranda puts it, any story of a person who comes from nearly nothing and reaches great success through his or her use of language is a hip-hop story.

Miranda accepted the 2016 Tony Award for best musical and the 2016 Pulitzer Prize for drama for his hip-hop musical, *Hamilton*.

advance, even as tickets sold for hundreds of dollars each. For a production intended to make America's story accessible to everyone, it sure was hard to get inside the theater. The production worked with the Rockefeller Foundation, which donated more than $7 million so thousands of students from New York City and other cities across the country could see the show.[1] As part of that privilege, students spent time on lessons about history, theater, and hip-hop. They created their own scenes, songs, and raps about parts of early American history that spoke to them.

Hip-Hop Is Art

Some people have been critical of bringing hip-hop into the classroom as an educational tool. Some critics claim it doesn't seem old enough to be a "real" art form. The attitude, ways of speaking, and posture of hip-hop have

First Lady Michelle Obama invited the cast of *Hamilton* to perform in the East Room of the White House on March 14, 2016.

sometimes been viewed as informal and unworthy of study. For years, this mind-set considered rappers gangsters and thugs, and it kept hip-hop dance moves on the streets or in clubs. Often, these dances were appropriated and marketed to mainstream culture, rather than honored as their own forms of art.

But these misconceptions have changed. As the hip-hop fans and practitioners of the late 1970s, 1980s, and certainly 1990s, such as Miranda, grew up, the dance moves they knew so well made their way into more widespread settings. Boys and girls brought their dance styles to studios, classrooms, and stages. In the process, they made changes and created New School hip-hop. Dance has always been changing, and this evolution is just another part of the art's development. Hip-hop dance is now viewed as a serious art form and is studied as such.

Hip-Hop Dance as Art

Hamilton uses the language and movement of hip-hop, as well as a multiracial cast, to present sights and sounds people recognize as conversational. Because of this, the audience sees familiar names from American history not as white marble, as often seen in school textbooks, but as relatable human beings. Thomas Jefferson, who sports a glorious Afro, is a lively character, not an antique painting. This relatability helps connect the actions of American history to the present and to our lives today. The ensemble uses a variety of dance styles, from ballet and jitterbug to tap and, of course, hip-hop's many forms. The dancers even incorporate furniture, including a sizable writing desk,

> "It's a story about America then, told by what America looks like now."[3]
>
> —Lin-Manuel Miranda

lifting it over their heads as though it has joined the dance. Even the stage itself is made to move, with three turning platforms built as a bull's-eye in the center.

Hamilton's economic triumph, as well as its success in captivating the dominant American popular culture, is unprecedented. Why is it so successful? The show's award-winning choreographer, Andy Blankenbuehler, believes the show's message resonates in today's political and cultural climate: "Hip-hop gives a sense of expression to humongous groups of people who are struggling with social injustices," he says. Hamilton is already inspiring a new generation of artists, Blankenbuehler offers, showing them "real stories can be told in new ways. Important stories can be told through dance, important stories can be told through rap."[4] This is something the leaders and followers of hip-hop have known for years. Hamilton's mash-up of the nation's founding "dead white guys" (and girls) with passionate lyrics and hip-hop dance means Broadway will never be the same.

What we today recognize as elements of hip-hop dance grew out of some popular dance moves of the 1960s and 1970s. They started in economically challenged, predominantly African-American and Puerto Rican urban neighborhoods in places such as Brooklyn and the Bronx

Hamilton has revolutionized how audiences view Broadway productions.

in New York City, and areas of Los Angeles and San Francisco in California. It is fitting, then, that the story of Alexander Hamilton, much of which takes place in New York, should be told in a verbal and physical language that was, in part, born there.

2 HIP-HOP DANCE
ORIGINS

The term *hip-hop* has generally come to mean the culture—consisting of music, lyrics, art, and dance—developed by urban youth, especially African-American and Puerto Rican youth, in the late 1900s. Hip-hop dance isn't a single style. Instead, it is a collection of many different styles from many backgrounds. Most of what is recognized as hip-hop dance today developed in the late 1960s and 1970s. Long before that, though, many different cultures danced in ways that influenced hip-hop. Some of these cultural practices had a part in how American dance evolved. Other dance styles are similar only by coincidence.

The Nicholas brothers, Harold and Fayard, combined tap, ballet, and acrobatic moves to create their own energetic style of dance in the 1930s.

Diverse Origins

Hip-hop dance found its origins in diverse US dance styles that mixed African, Caribbean, and Middle Eastern dance. For centuries, in cultures around the world, dancers have formed circles. The ancient Greeks, Middle Eastern groups, and African groups all formed circles around featured dancers. Some historians compare this practice to the ring of bystanders formed for hip-hop dancers, called a cypher. For the ancient Celts in Ireland, when celebrating, this circle turned clockwise; when mourning, the circle turned counterclockwise. Some dances also called for stopping in place and tapping the foot repeatedly. Both of these practices are still seen today in Irish step dancing, one of the precursors of tap dancing.

Tap dancing, in turn, is one of the precursors of hip-hop. It developed in the United States in the 1800s, though the term *tap dancing* wasn't used until 1903. In many ways, early tap came from the energetic, vigorous dance styles practiced in enslaved communities, which inherited some of their dance styles from Africa.

In the early 1800s, theatrical variety shows began touring the country. They featured actors, musicians, and some dancing. Show troupes began hiring mostly

Enslaved Africans brought their tribal rhythms and dances to American and Caribbean colonies, as shown in this period image.

male dancers who could impress an audience. The first American to achieve fame as a dancer, John Durang, was famous for his jigs. Then Thomas Dartmouth "Daddy" Rice created a character he named "Jim Crow," a caricature of an elderly African-American man. Rice's Jim Crow performed a type of jig—a footwork-heavy style—but also used his arms and hands. The dance was unlike any white audiences had seen. Rice's character became so popular it created a whole new genre of theater: minstrel shows.

JIGS

The percussive style of dance popularized in minstrel shows spread. In the 1840s, showman P. T. Barnum hired a percussive dancer named John Diamond. Diamond drew his dance moves from African-American, Irish, and English styles, and he supposedly won every dance competition he entered. Later, Barnum replaced him with William Henry Lane, an African-American man from New York City. Barnum had his new dancer paint himself with the same blackface makeup that white performers used, and billed him as "Master Juba." Juba is said to have been the first tap dancer. He was enormously popular.

Dance Styles Collide

Juba had learned his unique and eclectic style of tap dance in the melting-pot culture of New York's Five Points neighborhood. In urban neighborhoods generally, different groups that might otherwise keep to themselves tend to mingle with each other. In New York, European immigrants and African Americans were often

Jim Crow was a racially insensitive character with a signature dance, created by actor T. D. Rice in the 1830s.

JIM CROW,

Pub. by Hodgson, 10 Fleet Street & Turner & Fisher New York & Philadelphia

JIM CROW

"Daddy" Rice, a white actor, grew up among whites and blacks in the North in the 1810s and 1820s. He based the exaggerated mannerisms and speech patterns of his buffoonish Jim Crow character on those of African Americans he knew and of enslaved people he met in the South. Rice colored his face and hands black (though he was probably not the first white performer to do so) and wore ragged clothing. In addition to dancing, he told jokes in a rough dialect. Rice claimed he had learned the dance from an African-American man. Decades later, the term *Jim Crow* came to describe the system of laws, policies, and institutions that treated African Americans as less worthy than whites. That, not Rice's character, is what *Jim Crow* means today.

marginalized by native-born whites. They were of low social status and often struggled with poverty. In this atmosphere, Irish step dancers learned from their African-American neighbors, and African Americans learned from others as well. Different music and dance styles influenced each other.

African dances often call for the dancers to bend, hunch over, or simply relax their posture. In Irish dancing, as in most European dance styles, the upper body is held, if not rigid, at least upright. In tap dancing, which combines the two, the body is loose, the arms swing, and the dancer uses his or her whole body. But one of the greatest similarities between African dance and tap (as well as hip-hop styles) is improvisation. Certain moves can be taught, but performances are often put together on the spot.

Attitude, too, connects hip-hop, tribal dances from Africa, and tap. While European dances generally emphasize the first and third beats of a measure, African dances often stress the second and fourth. This creates a laid-back feeling most commonly found in jazz and swing music. Both of these styles later influenced hip-hop. Similarly, in African dance, as in hip-hop and tap, nonchalance—a calm, cool, unfazed attitude—is valued. If dancers really want to impress, they act as though their best moves are effortless.

Dancing for a Good Time

For thousands of years, dancing was one of the primary ways people entertained themselves

CAPOEIRA AND HIP-HOP: NO REAL CONNECTION

Some people claim hip-hop, particularly breaking, also came from a Brazilian martial arts form called capoeira. The two are both based on rhythm and share some moves, and both can sometimes be used to resolve disputes without physical contact. Some of the more acrobatic moves of hip-hop might resemble those in capoeira, but the martial arts practice didn't appear in New York until after hip-hop dance styles were already developed. The two may be connected in some communities today, but in the origins of hip-hop, there was no link between the two.

and dated. Music and dance clubs, dance contests, and get-togethers were everywhere and were attended by nearly everyone. Certain dance styles went in and out of fashion along with music. This was especially true before the invention of radio and television.

In the 1920s, known as the Roaring '20s, the foxtrot, waltz, and Charleston dances were in. During the 1930s, the Great Depression made life glum for many, but dancing was an outlet, a way to blow off steam without spending a lot of money. Dance styles during these decades were increasingly influenced by African-American culture, with musicians such as Cab Calloway at the forefront and dance moves including the Lindy Hop and the Big Apple starting out in black communities before spreading elsewhere. In the 1940s, during and after World War II (1939–1945), jazz, tap, and swing music heavily influenced popular culture, and professional ballroom dancing appeared.

By the 1950s, swing had been diverging into regional variations for three decades and featured a wide range of dance moves. But regional variations soon gave way to a nationalizing force: television. In 1957, the afternoon program *Bandstand* based in Philadelphia, Pennsylvania, went national under the name *American Bandstand*.

Cab Calloway was one of the most popular entertainers of the 1930s and 1940s.

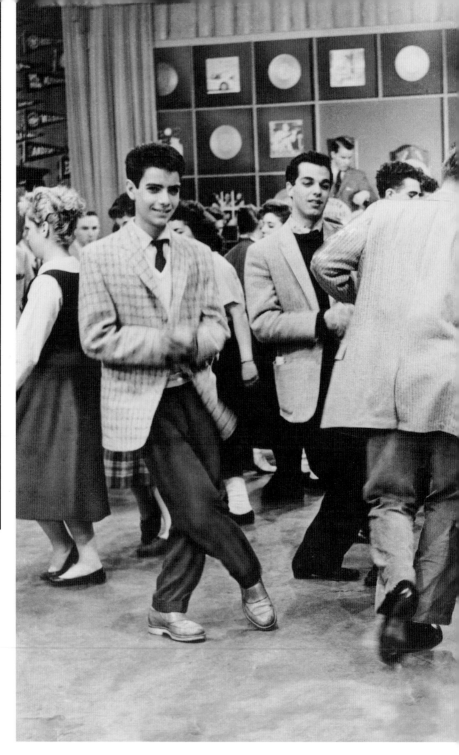

Hosted by Dick Clark, *American Bandstand* featured teens dancing popular dances of the time.

Suddenly, teens across the country were copying the same dances. In 1960, Americans took to the new dance, the Twist, in a huge way. The next decade would see a decrease in popular partner dances and a rise in songs with specific dances accompanying them.

Although hip-hop dance brings these many influences together, it wasn't developed by professional or formally trained dancers. Most of the earliest breakers, poppers, and lockers knew moves only from social settings or television shows. Yet, as it happened, even this training could go a long way.

3 LOCKING AND POPPING

Dance is a social activity. In the ages before television, and for years after its invention, dancing was an opportunity to have fun and meet new people. Your moves may change depending on whom you are with. You may dance differently in front of your parents than at a party with your friends. People might judge your ability to dance. But one thing is for sure: just watching other people dance isn't as much fun as joining in.

With the rise of television, though, came an increasing number of fad, or novelty, dances. This is the kind of dance that goes with a particular song. The song may be popular for only a brief time, such as PSY's 2012 "Gangnam

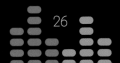

Locking and popping pioneer and teacher PopMaster Fabel is part of the
Rock Steady Crew.

Style." Or, it might stick around for years, such as the Macarena. In the 1960s, fad dances were everywhere. If you were around then, you'd have done the Shimmy, the Mashed Potato, or the Watusi. You might even have tried the Funky Chicken.

JAMES BROWN'S INFLUENCE

James Brown is considered the "Godfather of Soul," but his influence on hip-hop dance cannot be denied. He started out as a gospel singer but quickly turned his focus to other musical forms. Brown's live performances electrified audiences. He did dances no one had ever seen before—daring, athletic moves. He was called the "Hardest-Working Man in Showbiz," not just because he toured constantly, but because his performances were far beyond any other singer's. A number of classic dance moves are inspired by steps that James Brown developed on his own. Michael Jackson's Moonwalk, for example, is a descendant of James Brown's Camel Walk. The Boogaloo, adopted and adapted by hip-hop founders, is a James Brown move.

It was in this landscape of popular social dances that hip-hop dance emerged. Breaking, popping, locking, tutting (featuring arm movements inspired by ancient Egyptian art), and a variety of other styles arose on dance floors. According to one of the earliest hip-hop dancers, Richard "Crazy Legs" Colón, their creation was sparked by James Brown's music and dance, and by the dancers' own competitive natures.

Richard "Crazy Legs" Colón formed the Rock Steady Crew, the first professional hip-hop dance crew.

If You Can't Dance, Invent

Although the Funky Chicken was a popular dance for many years, in the late 1960s in Los Angeles, a young man named Don Campbell had some difficulty perfecting it. In fact, he wasn't a very good dancer at all. He would stop and start, trying to remember a move or think of what to do next. But he kept trying. In 1969, Campbell made the dance his own and began incorporating his jerks and locking joints intentionally. No longer was he doing the Funky Chicken. He wasn't even inventing a new dance move. He was inventing a brand-new style of dance.

The beat of the music is what gets dancers and audiences moving together. Campbell's style of locking, which included halting stops between moves, visually illustrated and emphasized the beat. And although it was initially something of an accident, this style quickly became popular. Some performers even added acrobatics to their dances. They used jumps, flips, and tucks. They dropped into half splits, butt drops, and knee drops. And, of course, they showed off their complex step patterns and fancy footwork.

> "Locking is not a battle dance. It's a party dance. It's a dance that was made up to have fun, to uplift people."[1]
>
> —Flomaster, professional dancer

Don Campbell created locking, which he showed off at the 2005 Choreographer's Ball.

Within three or four years, Don Campbell and others who had learned his style formed a dance group called the Lockers. The dancers had nicknames and named their

dances after themselves. The Lockers dressed in brightly colored clothing, pushing fashion almost to the point of being silly. Jeff Chang's book *Total Chaos* explains how Campbell and his friends did "the lock, points, skeeters, scooby doos, stop 'n' go, which-away, and the fancies."[2]

HIP-HOP DANCE REACHES MILLIONS

With the rise of television dance shows, regional differences between dance moves and styles were beginning to disappear. *American Bandstand*, for example, could see the same dance moves done by different people each week. This, and other dance shows similar to it, featured popular dance groups, but it wasn't just dance shows that featured these famous guests. The Lockers also appeared on mainstream programs, including *The Tonight Show*, *The Dick Van Dyke Show*, *The Carol Burnett Show*, and *Saturday Night Live*. With these appearances, they reached enormous audiences.

If Your Dancing Has Glitches

Just a few years after locking developed, the dance scene would see its next new style in Fresno, California: popping. While locking includes repeated freezes, popping smooths over those freezes, minimizing them to a percussive jerk in one part of the body. When done well, popping can make a dancer look like a video with glitches.

Inspired by the Jerk, Chubby Checker's Twist, and James Brown's Popcorn,

Boogaloo Sam, *left*, and Don Campbell, *right*, spoke about dance trends at the 2010 World Hip Hop Dance Championship.

"Boogaloo Sam" Solomon developed the new style he called popping around 1975. Within a year, Boogaloo Sam and his brother, Timothy "Popin' Pete" Solomon, formed a dance group called the Electronic Boogaloo Lockers (later, the Electric Boogaloos). The members of this group had learned how to dance from watching dance shows on television and admiring groups such as the Lockers.

But they didn't just copy what they saw. They also added their own techniques, such as popping, and even some gymnastic flips. The Electric Boogaloo performed on *Soul Train*, a dance show similar to *American Bandstand*.

Popping is stylistically very similar to locking. The styles are so similar that many people call both dance forms "pop-locking" or "popping and locking," but dancers will tell you it is physically impossible to do both at the same time. In fact, popping is sometimes used to refer to a wide variety of dance styles from the West Coast. But according to Popin' Pete, "There are people who wave and there are people who tut. They're not popping."[3]

SOUL TRAIN

The television dance show *Soul Train* began in Chicago, Illinois, in 1970. It aired nationally in 1971. Produced by Don Cornelius, *Soul Train* changed the landscape of popular dance and brought music styles that were considered mostly African American to a large white audience. The show ended in 2006, after 35 years and more than 1,100 episodes.[4] Cornelius admitted that he found some aspects of hip-hop and rap upsetting, but he understood that they were important to his fans.

Do the Boogaloo

The boogaloo is a dance style very similar to popping. Boogaloo style uses every part of the body and involves sharp angles—such as knees and elbows, rotating hips, and knees twisting out from the body. Boogaloo Sam helped develop this style.

Popin' Pete describes it as "moving the body continuously in different directions."[5] Their group, the Electric Boogaloo, helped popularize the boogaloo as well as popping.

Together, popping, locking, and roboting are called funk styles. Although television dance shows in some ways helped unify styles nationally, there were still strong regional differences. Dancers on the West Coast were culturally different from the dancers of New York City in the 1970s, just as Californians and New Yorkers today have some cultural differences. The funk styles began separately from each other and from New York dance and, for the most part, also grew and changed separately.

> "Popping, besides the mechanics of it, is a dance to be cool. How illusionary and unreal can I be? When you're popping, the idea is that it's not possible."[6]
>
> —Bradley Rapier, dancer, choreographer, and founder of the Groovaloos

Even so, as popular culture began absorbing hip-hop dance, music, and attitude in the 1980s, these very different dance styles were often lumped together under the larger heading of "hip-hop dance," along with breaking. The styles' originators still knew what was what, but those outside the culture referred to everything as break dancing, even though that term describes a single

Soul Train focused on African-American dance, funk, and soul.

dance style from the Bronx. The men and women of the West Coast dance scene, according to Rennie Harris, a hip-hop dancer and choreographer, "got swallowed up by hip-hop . . . when they had never heard of it."[7]

4 BREAKING IN THE
BRONX

For some, hip-hop dance brings to mind people on flattened cardboard boxes, spinning on their feet, their heads, and their backs. A circle of dancers await their turn, as each member of the crew shows his or her best moves. They show off acrobatics and gymnastics, all in time to a huge silver boom box with a cassette tape deck—or maybe just a big old radio.

In reality, this is only one kind of hip-hop dance, and it has changed quite a bit over the years. Popping and locking, among other styles, are separate and distinct from breaking, although more and more dancers combine the moves. Breaking—or as it was called by outsiders in the 1980s, break dancing—may

Breakers are most often recognized by their acrobatic and creative moves.

be the most well-known of these styles, and it is done all around the world. But breaking all started in the Bronx, a borough of New York City, in the 1970s.

Location: The Bronx

New York in the 1970s was, for many, a hard place to live, and the Bronx was the poorest part of the city in many ways. Gangs were active, made up of young men and women hoping for friendship and safety in numbers. Gangs protected their members and their territory. Some of these young people competed by dancing.

These dances were done with a partner—though that partner is better called an opponent. Opponents might use complicated or very current dance moves to claim superiority. These usually exhausting dances allowed rivals, whether individuals or gangs, to safely settle a dispute.

> "A lot of things in early hip-hop were like chitlins—the stuff that was largely cast away, but then poor folk took hold of it and made it a dynamic part of the musical diet."[1]
>
> —*Michael Eric Dyson*, Know What I Mean?: Reflections on Hip-Hop

By the late 1960s and early 1970s, the competitive style used in Brooklyn was called uprocking. Breaking developed in the Bronx around the same time, and in some ways was influenced by

Breaking was a fun, safe alternative to street violence in the Bronx.

A b-boy in Atlanta, Georgia, takes to the middle of the cypher to show off his skills.

uprock, although it kept a separate identity. The purpose of uprocking is to settle disputes and illustrate superiority, but breaking is less battle focused. B-boys and b-girls—as breakers are called—compete by taking turns to show off their best moves, rather than dancing at the same time as their opponent.

Hip-hop music and dance created a neutral ground for competitive young people seeking an outlet for their energy. Early DJs, such as Kool Herc and Afrika Bambaataa, began hosting jams in community centers and common rooms of housing projects, and later in clubs—and even in the streets—and inviting everyone. These parties brought people from different neighborhoods together in a safe and neutral space. Many young people formed dance crews and competed with others. Dance gave them a strenuous but safe social outlet.

Looping the Break

It was at a party deejayed by Kool Herc in 1973 that breaking as a style first began. The break is the part of a song when the melody and harmony pause and the sound is pared down to the rhythm section—bass and percussion. Playing old records from artists such as James Brown, Herc realized the dancers were always waiting for the break. So he started looping a song's break, using two record players with the same record on both. He played the break on one and then the same break on the other. This technique is called the merry-go-round, and it allows for just a few seconds of music to run for several minutes. Once Herc started looping the breaks, nobody wanted to go back to

A DANCER'S SET

Most dancers reference certain rules of engagement. First, they step into the cypher, formed by bystanders. Next, a b-boy or b-girl starts by showing his or her toprock moves, followed by footwork, a power move, and then a freeze. A full set is around half a minute, and it's the freeze—a position or pose that is held—that punctuates it. Here, dancers can be completely creative. A freeze might respond to the previous dancer's freeze. It might involve a friend or two. Of course, not all dancers follow these rules, and certainly not every time they dance.

listening to the whole record. Dancers gradually stopped doing group dances, instead taking turns to show off their best moves. Herc called these dancers "break boys," which was then shortened to "b-boys."

As the 1970s wore on, breaking changed. Initially, the emphasis of breaking had been on the beat, but it began shifting to flashy power moves. Gymnastic and even acrobatic moves became more popular, and dancers began to spin two, three, or more times in a row—on their hands, their knees, and even their heads.

Mainstream culture's first introduction to hip-hop came with the Sugarhill Gang's 1979 hit "Rapper's Delight." As rap music increased in popularity throughout the 1980s, hip-hop dance also gained popularity in mainstream culture. The many funk styles of the West Coast were lumped together with breaking from New York and commercialized under the name "break dancing." Dance groups such as the Rock Steady Crew became popular and began touring.

BREAKING
DOWN BREAKING

There are several varieties of breaking. Toprock is the most similar to uprock, in that it is done completely while standing. Intended to show speed and agility, toprock is influenced by a variety of dance styles, including uprock, tap, Lindy Hop, Native American and African tribal dances, and even older American styles, such as the Charleston, popular in the 1920s. Initially, toprock made up a large part of a b-boy's or b-girl's routine, but over time, as floor rocking became a larger part of breaking, toprock became just an introductory section of the dance. By the 1980s, anyone who used mainly toprock in battles was viewed as old-fashioned.

Floor rock, sometimes called downrock, is the dancing a b-boy or b-girl does from the ground, generally supported by the arms. The switch from toprocking to floor rocking is known as the drop. Front swipes, back swipes, dips, and corkscrews are different kinds of drops. Whatever you call it, whether ground work, floor rock, or downrock, this part of the dance is generally a collection of power moves. Power moves include spins, such as on the hands (known as floats), or on the head, knee, butt, or back, as well as other acrobatic maneuvers.

The basic toprock move involves crossing one leg forward in front of the other and then switching to do the same with the other foot.

violence. Rather than brawling, youth could demonstrate their superiority with a better performance, the winner to be determined by bystanders. But this sort of street battle did not begin with hip-hop.

Deep Roots of Hip-Hop

In the 1700s, enslaved Africans in New York City, when and if they could find a few spare moments, might stop by one of Manhattan's markets to dance for a few coins. Competition rose between enslaved people living in the

Youth took their hip-hop performances to the streets in 1984.

city and those from the country. This street dance tradition continued. With dance styles that valued speed and technique as well as creativity, competitions occurred naturally.

This competitive spirit continued into the 1900s. In the 1930s, tap dancers challenged each other, particularly on the streets of Philadelphia. Before you could hang out with the crowd on a particular street corner, you had to be able to meet its level of dance skill. Even in the 1950s, teenagers (whether in gangs or not) danced competitively in the street. Two decades later, in the 1970s, the practice had become somewhat different in style, but the differences were small. The music changed, too, from swing to funk to hip-hop, and the dance styles changed along with the music.

PHILADELPHIA'S RENNIE HARRIS

Lorenzo "Rennie" Harris grew up in Philadelphia. Inspired by Don Campbell and the Lockers, Harris started creating dance crews as a teenager. He founded the Scanner Boys, a group that helped bring hip-hop culture to Philadelphia in the early 1980s. In 1992, he founded Puremovement, a dance company that provides classes, workshops, mentoring programs, and lectures on hip-hop history. Harris is dedicated to keeping hip-hop culture and all it stands for alive.

Let's See Your Moves

As the dance styles that would later grow into hip-hop became popular in the 1960s and 1970s, young people took to trying to best each other in dance. The b-boys and b-girls in these crews were often from the same neighborhood, and they sought to be part of a crew for friendship and security. New dancers learned from those who had more experience, and everybody was encouraged to be creative and show their individuality through dance.

Because both crews and gangs are groups of young people, some people outside of hip-hop culture often thought breaking itself was a sign of violence. While tensions could run high at dance battles, dances were generally safe gatherings. DJ Kool Herc, for example, enforced a strict policy of nonviolence in his block parties. Dance crew leaders became role models, focusing on respect through dance skill rather than violence.

> "I think hip-hop has bridged the culture gap. It brings white kids together with black kids, brown kids with yellow kids. They all have something in common that they love. It gets past the stereotypes."[1]
>
> —DJ Kool Herc

The Rock Steady Crew performs outside of the Booker T. Washington Junior High School in New York in 1983.

Hip-Hop Goes Pro

In 1977, a group called the Rock Steady Crew formed possibly the first professional hip-hop dance crew. Unlike

most other crews, the members of Rock Steady came from

across New York City, not just one neighborhood. Richard

"Crazy Legs" Colón was only 11 years old when he became

a founding member of the group. Roughly a decade after hip-hop began, Crazy Legs came up as part of the second generation. By this time, breaking was becoming less popular in the African-American community where it began, and new Latino and Latina dancers were introducing more acrobatic moves. The Rock Steady Crew is still dancing in the 2010s, but Crazy Legs is the only founding member who is still involved. Most of the others have gone on to other careers, though a few of them, including Crazy Legs, still teach dance to local kids.

Six years after its formation in 1977, the Rock Steady Crew joined Afrika Bambaataa, the Fantastic Four double Dutch girls, and other hip-hop stars in a performance tour in Europe. With them came rappers,

INFLUENCE ON LATINO HIP-HOP

It is nearly impossible to imagine hip-hop dance—or hip-hop itself—without Latinos and Latinas. The Rock Steady Crew was led by a Puerto Rican New Yorker, Richard Colón. Actress and choreographer Rosie Perez, born to Puerto Rican parents in Brooklyn, started dancing professionally as a college student in Los Angeles. Soon she was a featured dancer on *Soul Train*. She choreographed *In Living Color*, an influential comedy show that aired from 1990 to 1994. Jennifer Lopez, also from New York City, got her start as one of the Fly Girls, dancers on *In Living Color*. Her recording career reflects the merging of Latino, hip-hop, R&B, soul, and pop music.

graffiti artists, and other dancers. By this time, b-boys and b-girls could be found from Japan to Italy, and from Germany to Hawaii. Just the year before, Dance System #10, another dance crew, toured South America and the Caribbean and performed at Madison Square Garden in New York. Members of Dance System #10 were between 11 and 15 years old at the time. The young ages of the performers highlighted the youthful energy of the culture in general, even as it spread hip-hop internationally.

Hip-Hop Dance on Television

Breaking made it into movies and television in the early 1980s. It was often featured for a brief moment in the background, such as in the 1983 movie *Flashdance*. In the PBS documentary *Style Wars*, however, breaking was the focus of the production. Some b-boys and b-girls worried that these films ignored the hip-hop culture that accompanied breaking. The social issues to which hip-hop was a reaction—such as poverty

B-GIRL ASIA ONE

B-girl Asia One is a legend who first became interested in hip-hop in the 1980s. She began breaking in 1991 and even trained with the Rock Steady Crew. She founded B-Boy Summit in 1994. This event brings performances, workshops, and panels together to showcase hip-hop dance, music, art, and overall culture.

The Beat Freaks, an all-female dance crew, appeared on season three of MTV's *America's Best Dance Crew* in 2009.

and racial discrimination—often did not make it into the final cut. But even though some of the culture around

hip-hop dance may have been lost in translation, its rise in popularity helped ensure the style would not disappear.

6
FAD AND PARTY
DANCES

Hip-hop, similar to every other musical genre, has its own history of fad dances—dances that sweep the scene and are wildly popular for a short period of time. They're everywhere and then seem to fade away after a few months. But they leave their imprints on whatever comes next.

Dance crazes often have funny or clever names, or just sound silly. The Mashed Potato. The Peppermint Twist. The Frug (pronounced "froog"). The Watusi. Sometimes the crazes are born out of a specific song, and the song's lyrics explain how to do the dance, such as Little Eva's "The Loco-Motion" in 1962 or Cupid's "Cupid Shuffle" in 2007. Sometimes a fad dance is just

a pattern of movement that isn't necessarily connected to one particular song but rather to a rhythm or musical feeling. "The Hustle" is a song with its own dance, but people dance the Hustle to many different songs because it is easy and fun, and why not?

From Fad to Party Standard

Some dance crazes stick around, in fits and starts, long after the initial burst of enthusiasm has died down. The most long-lived fad dances become almost hokey standards, dances that even grandmas do at their own birthday parties. Many people have been to parties and weddings where every person in the room, old and young, got up and did the Electric Slide, which was popular in the early 1990s. Many people believe the Electric Slide dance was invented then, but the truth is that it got its start decades before. "Electric Boogie" was

DO THE SILLY THING

Many names for dances come straight from the name of the song the dance goes with—such as the 1960s dances the Twist and the Loco-Motion, and the Hustle and the Bus Stop from the 1970s. But a lot of fad dance names seem to have come out of thin air. Recently, hip-hop has brought us the Nae-Nae and the Laffy Taffy. Chickens, which do look like they're dancing when they strut around a henhouse, come up often in dance names: from James Brown's Funky Chicken to the Chicken Head and Chicken Noodle Soup.

a Marcia Griffiths hit in 1976. The dance went along with the song even then.

Many hip-hop dance moves are riffs on steps developed by dancers a generation or two before. Over time, dancers take old moves, add some new pops and twists, and refine them, and the dances become something new. It's a physical version of musical sampling, done on the dance floor instead of in the recording studio. Choreographer Jamaica Craft and hip-hop dancer Sione Kelepi described the Shmoney, a 2013 dance craze, as having a little bit of James Brown's Camel Walk in it. James Brown did the Camel Walk back in the 1960s. It shows that steps go in and out of fashion, but they never go away completely.

How many times have people lined up at a party to recreate the classic Michael Jackson "Thriller" dance? Roboting, or the Robot, is a hip-hop dance Michael Jackson pioneered in the 1970s. Today it is one of the most recognizable dance moves. The dancer

THE ELECTRIC SLIDE

The Electric Slide is a line dance that has become a party standard. It is enjoyed by dancers of all ages. As with many fad dances, the Electric Slide has several versions, some more complicated than others. Complex versions have more than 20 steps, but almost any dancer—young or old—can quickly learn the basic dance, which has 16 steps.

On Halloween 2016, thousands of people dressed as zombies participated in the choreographed "Thriller" dance at Universal Studios in Japan.

moves to the beat of the music, stopping his or her body and locking it in place to emulate the jerky moves of a robot. The Robot is a part of so many hip-hop dances, so constantly used in freestyle dance and subgenres, that it is like the letter *e* in the English alphabet—even if we don't think about it, it's everywhere.

Everybody Get On Board

Over the years, many new hip-hop dance fads spread after being featured on television dance shows. *Soul Train* was

the most influential of the television dance shows. The dancers, most of whom were professionals, showed off the latest fashion trends, but the important thing was the moves. On *Soul Train*, hip-hop fans saw dances such as the Harlem Shake (which became huge in 2001) and the Lean Back, with its heyday in the summer of 2004. In addition to dance shows, variety shows such as *In Living Color* in the 1990s, and later, websites such as YouTube, brought hip-hop dancing into homes across the United States.

Line Dances

Many party dances are line dances. Often, people associate the phrase *line dance* with country music, but many hip-hop dances are line dances, too, such as the Cupid Shuffle or the Booty Call. The crucial factor isn't the musical genre but rather the way the dance is performed. A line dance is a dance in which performers line up and do not touch each other. There are no permanent partners. Instead, everyone moves in sync with each other to create a choreographed whole. Line dancing is the opposite of freestyle. There may be some leeway in the details of a performance, but when a group of people are performing a specific dance, their movements will generally, and maybe very precisely, match.

The Whip/Nae-Nae is a dance craze that is often performed as a line dance. Inspired by a character on the

Boston City Councilor Tito Jackson teaches a crowd the Cupid Shuffle in 2015.

Fox sitcom *Martin,* the dance involves swinging one's torso and hips and whipping one's arms out. Silentó's single "Watch Me"—the song that goes with the dance— isn't particularly fast and doesn't seem like a song that would require a lot of physical effort to dance to. But the words of the song tell another story. "Watch me Whip, watch me Nae-Nae," Silentó raps. He then goes on to tell his listeners to do the Stanky Leg, the Bop, the Yule, and the Superman. It's like an update of the old Wilson Pickett song "Land of a Thousand Dances" (1966), which tells the dancers to do the Pony, the Mashed Potato, the Watusi, the Alligator, and the Jerk.

The cultural reach of the Nae-Nae is vast. Actors, musicians, and comedians have performed it; football players use it as a victory dance; and President Barack Obama once mentioned being impressed by a video of a Washington, DC, police officer performing it in a spontaneous dance-off with some local teenagers.

Hip-hop dance is the kind of dancing that brings people together. It is sometimes competitive, requiring real skill and strength to be good at some of these moves, but it is mostly loose and forgiving enough that anyone with a mind to do it can enjoy the groove and just dance. Dance crazes may seem silly and unimportant, but as

During the 2016 Pro Bowl, Seattle Seahawks player Michael Bennett danced the Whip/Nae-Nae with a mascot.

any music fan knows, they're not, and they never entirely fade away.

BEHIND
THE SONG

WATCH ME

In 2015, "Watch Me (Whip/Nae-Nae)" by Silentó seemed to be playing everywhere, and the Whip/Nae-Nae—the dance that went with it—was everywhere as well. In fact, the song mentions seven different dance moves, most of them previously not well-known outside of the dance and hip-hop communities. But the moves are easy for anyone to learn. Here are a few:

The Whip: Step to the side so your feet are more than shoulder width apart. Make a fist and push that arm straight out in front of you. Hold it there and bounce your knees.

The Nae-Nae: Set your feet wide, angled outward. Hold one hand high, with your palm open. With your other arm angled down, sway or rock your body from side to side.

Break your legs: Put your feet together, with knees bent and hips and arms loose. Bend your knees from side to side.

Bop: Keeping your feet apart again, shake your knees in and out to the beat. Put one fist down in front of you and the other down behind you for two beats; then switch your hands.

Remember, hip-hop dance is all about improvisation and creativity. Make changes. Use these dances in other ways or for other purposes. And be yourself!

Silentó danced the Whip/Nae-Nae while arriving at the 2015 BET Awards.

7

SCHOOL

With new individuals from new communities learning and developing new styles for various audiences, change in hip-hop was, and is, inevitable. A significant development for hip-hop dance in particular, and hip-hop culture in general, was the incorporation of hip-hop styles in academic settings. Even though groups such as the Rock Steady Crew and Dance System #10 were performing in huge venues in the 1980s, from Madison Square Garden in New York City to Vauxhall in London, these performances were still thought by many to be novelty acts.

Hip-hop wasn't developed by academics with a background in musical theory. It was

n the 1990s, artists such as MC Hammer incorporated hip-hop dance in

created by men and women who felt a rhythm and were inspired to move. Having just begun in the 1960s and 1970s, hip-hop was for years considered a fad, not real dancing. But hip-hop practitioners knew it wasn't a fad and that hip-hop wasn't going away.

The Spread of Street Dance

The presence of breaking, popping, locking, and other styles on television may not have convinced schools or parents that hip-hop was real. But the huge popularity of music videos in the 1980s helped hip-hop spread, just as dance shows had done in previous years. Fad dances continued to arise, and in the 1980s and 1990s, the dances that accompanied certain songs could be conveyed far more quickly. Years later, in the 2010s, young people can use the Internet to find those same videos and newer ones just like them, all of which spread hip-hop styles even faster. It became easier and easier over time to create new trends in dance, such as Walk It Out, Chicken Noodle Soup, and Teach Me How to Dougie. With video-sharing sites such as YouTube, those

> "Hip hop is still in embryo, I mean, I have been doing this for 30 years but it is still a baby compared with other dance forms."[1]
>
> —Popin' Pete, a hip-hop dance founder

who wanted to learn dances were able to do so regardless of whom they knew or where the nearest popper or b-boy was.

And then there were feature films. In the 1980s, films such as *Breakin'* and the hit *Flashdance* portrayed hip-hop dance as a fad or even just part of the backdrop. But hip-hop dance took center stage in several movies of the early 2000s, such as *Save the Last Dance* (2001), *Step Up* (2006), and *Stomp the Yard* (2007). A variety of other films, while not focused solely on hip-hop dance styles, incorporated them alongside other, more established dances. These movies include *Happy Feet* and *Footloose*. Television shows such as *So You Think You Can Dance* (which premiered in 2005) and *America's Best Dance Crew* (which premiered in 2008) brought hip-hop dance into viewers' homes on a weekly basis.

Theater productions have been incorporating hip-hop dance techniques for years

HIP-HOP IS HERE TO STAY

In 2003, the Oxford English Dictionary included several hip-hop terms in its online updates, including "phat," "jiggy," and "breakbeat." In 2016, the New York Public Library acquired an archive of audio, video, and photographic resources about hip-hop. As well as being a useful research tool, this archive is a symbol that hip-hop is academically accepted as a formal dance style, akin to ballet and modern dance.

Movies such as *Step Up Revolution* (2012) bring hip-hop to audiences on the big screen, further cementing hip-hop dance in today's culture.

as well, but none until *Hamilton* have focused on hip-hop dance or culture, or achieved a level of success that brought hip-hop a larger audience. In 1986, the stage adaptation of a Charles Dickens story, *The Mystery of Edwin*

Drood, featured two hip-hop dancers, Steve Galvin and Mr. Wiggles. The production won several prestigious awards, but its influence by and on hip-hop was minimal. Given the success of hip-hop dance and rap music in

Lisa "Left Eye" Lopes of TLC performs the group's choreographed hit "No Scrubs" live at the 1999 MTV Video Music Awards.

general between the 1970s and 2010s, it is somewhat surprising there wasn't a wildly successful rap musical until 2015's *Hamilton*.

In 2002, Monsters of Hip-Hop became the first all-hip-hop dance convention. It has become a yearly event, with classes and competitions held nationally and, occasionally, internationally. For some, these conventions are an introduction to the world of dance, while for others, the conventions are an opportunity to brush up on their skills. In either case, Monsters of Hip-Hop brings new choreographers and dancers together.

Hip-Hop Gets Respect

Hip-hop dance can also be found in academic settings. Several colleges offer concentrations

HIP-HOP GOES TO SCHOOL

Rider University in New Jersey and Union College in Schenectady, New York, offer studio classes in hip-hop dance, along with ballet and jazz. Some programs such as these are led by founders of hip-hop dance. PopMaster Fabel, a member of the Rock Steady Crew, has taught workshops at Cornell University in Ithaca, New York, and has even brought in Crazy Legs Colón to teach some workshops of his own. From 2012 to 2015, Afrika Bambaataa was a visiting scholar at Cornell.

and minors in hip-hop. The University of Arizona allows students to concentrate on hip-hop as part of a minor in Africana Studies—a pen-and-paper kind of education in cultural studies, rather than physical education that focuses on dance and performance. In May 2015, the University of Southern California became the first major institution to dedicate an entire school to hip-hop. The Hip Hop School of Arts offers classes in b-boying/b-girling and deejaying, among other activities, not just to college students and adults, but also as an after-school program for boys and girls. The goal of the school is to provide young men and women with a safe alternative to some of the more dangerous activities of the streets.

Hip-hop dance moves rarely cause the same kind of uproar as do some of the more controversial, and even violent, lyrics of hip-hop music. Also, dance is exercise, and

Hip-hop dance classes are offered at community centers and colleges around the world, as seen here in Australia.

exercise is good for everyone. Across the country, dancers from the earlier years of hip-hop are starting programs for children and teens to learn to dance. In Lodi, California, Gabriela and Angelo Magdaleno started a group called the Inspiring Hope Community Dancers, offering classes in "street styles" to local children.

Commercialization

With hip-hop's increasing popularity in the 1980s came commercialization: buying and selling, and producing to sell. This includes studio hip-hop, which is more practiced and choreographed (as opposed to freestyle), and also many fad dance moves. Old School hip-hop dance forms, such as locking, are challenging and require a lot of practice to accomplish. As hip-hop grew in popularity in the 1980s and 1990s, dances became easier so more people could do them. In the 1990s, dances such as the Running Man and Robocop were moves the average person could do. Their success made hip-hop dance different from what it once was. And

> "The library is making a statement. Ballet, modern dance, tap—the library is placing hip hop culture on the same pedestals as other established dance movements."[2]
>
> —Michael Holman, videographer and promoter, on the New York Public Library's additions of hip-hop archives

In 2016, the Running Man challenge swept the world as people filmed their own versions of the Running Man and posted them on social media.

hip-hop dance didn't just influence other art forms; it was also influenced by them. Martial arts and reggae were among the many influences on hip-hop style. Hip-hop changed; it became more accepted as an art form, but it also entered a new phase of development among its practitioners. The sum of all these influences can be called New School. It has become so mainstream, the key question is no longer "Is it a real art form," but rather, "Is it authentic?"

A vital part of hip-hop culture has always been authenticity, or "keeping it real"—in other words, being true to street culture. It can be hard to define which dances are authentic and which are developed for publicity. The 2000s saw a number of novelty dances, such as that accompanying "Crank That" by Soulja Boy (DeAndre Way). Are they all in the true spirit of hip-hop dance, demonstrating physical ability and personal creativity?

Is dance still considered hip-hop when it's so mainstream that it is disconnected from the rest of hip-hop culture? What dances and songs keep hip-hop real? And who gets to decide? Only recently has the original generation of hip-hoppers begun to age. Is New School the end of hip-hop, or only the beginning?

Soulja Boy teaches actress Natalie Portman the dance moves to his song "Crank That" on MTV's *Total Request Live* in 2007.

8 AROUND THE WORLD

Though hip-hop dance never disappeared from the street and the studio, a television show from 2008 to 2012 brought b-boying and b-girling back into the limelight. *America's Best Dance Crew* was similar to *American Idol* and, in fact, was created by Randy Jackson, one of the *American Idol* judges. The show pitted several crews against each other, eliminating one crew per episode over the course of the season. Although the show did not last as long as *American Idol*, the dance crews involved were well aware that they were bringing breaking to many people who might not have any other experience with the style, and they tried to stay true to the culture of hip-hop.

The Jabbawockeez, known for wearing masks during their dances, were the winners of *America's Best Dance Crew* season one.

Far from being a brief fad, hip-hop dance has only grown over the last 30 years. In addition to popping, locking, and breaking, there are entirely new styles, such as Memphis jookin', krumping, and tutting. Tutting is

said to have been inspired by the style of Egyptian art. It is a dance style performed almost entirely in the arms, incorporating sharp angles at the wrists and elbows.

Hip-hop dance, whether it be breaking, popping, locking, or any of a number of styles, has always been intended to allow a dancer to display his or her creativity. This freestyle aspect has allowed for all sorts of physical arts to impact the dance—whether it be African or Native American tribal dances, jazz, Irish or English dance, or even martial arts such, as kung fu. Despite some debate as to what influenced the initial development of hip-hop in the United States, as hip-hop spread across the world, it was adapted by and for the men and women who practiced it.

Rise Up

Hip-hop was developed in underprivileged communities, largely by African Americans and Puerto Ricans. The style, the culture, and the dance didn't become multicultural—hip-hop began that way. It gave minority groups a way to express themselves and an

FINGER TUTTING

Finger tutting is, in effect, a scaled-down, more precise version of tutting. It focuses not on the whole arm, but on the hands and fingers. While Mark "King Boogaloo Tut" Benson is said to have developed and popularized tutting in the late 1970s, finger tutting is said to have developed in the late 1990s in New York. Finger Circus is a finger-tutting crew based in California. One of its members, John "P-Nut" Hunt, was featured in the music video for Taylor Swift's "Shake It Off." Another member, Chase "CTut" Lindsey, is credited with developing face tutting, which is finger tutting with the hands held before the face.

identity besides "other" or "not white." Hip-hop gave people a way to celebrate themselves, whatever their race, social or economic class, or gender—and it still does.

In Germany, many hip-hop dancers today are either immigrants or the children of immigrants—another underprivileged group in most societies. Team Recycled is a prominent dance crew on the German hip-hop scene in the 2010s, whose members are of African, Eastern European, Middle Eastern, and Asian descent. In the spirit of hip-hop, they have formed a surrogate family. "What holds us together is our passion for hip hop," says one member.[1] Many find hip-hop a way to protest the discrimination they experience as immigrants or nonwhite Germans.

Similarly, many of those in the hip-hop scene in France are immigrants or the children of immigrants. Farid Berki, a hip-hop dancer and choreographer, has described his background as fairly typical for the French hip-hop

KRUMPING

Krumping is dramatic, battle-based dancing. In many ways, it is one of the most impressive forms of dance. It requires tremendous strength, skill, and discipline. Dancers can improvise their moves on the floor, but the movements are highly controlled. Krumping can incorporate moves from many different kinds of dance. It is all about creative expression. *Rize*, a 2005 documentary film, illustrates krumping.

Krumpers make strong statements through dance.

scene: he grew up with a French mother and Algerian father, and he comes from an underprivileged background with little formal education. When hip-hop spread to France in the 1980s (mostly developed by French-speaking people of African and Caribbean descent), he taught himself to pop, lock, and break and also learned other dance styles.

> "Hip-hop culture gave a voice to the people in the society who weren't otherwise represented. . . . 'I am also here, listen to me.'"[3]
>
> —Falk Schacht, German music journalist and hip-hop artist

French hip-hop dance is supported within the French theater community. In 2005, Anne Nguyen, an expert in breaking and hip-hop battles, founded Compagnie par Terre. The company works to bring hip-hop styles and artists to the stage. Nguyen choreographs with influences from popping, waacking, and other styles, using hip-hop to tell stories as well as show emotion.

As hip-hop spread outward from the United States in the 1980s, it traveled west to Japan and caught on immediately. According to Junya Takahashi, president of the hip-hop company Movement, "Hip-hop dance has developed from a trend to a culture among the general public."[2] Japanese b-boys and b-girls from the first

The street dance group Maximum Crew is popular in South Korea.

generation now have children of their own, and they want to pass on the dance. In the last decade, Japanese education laws were reformed to require that both martial arts and dance be included as part of physical education. It is up to each school to decide how long students will spend on dance, and schools may choose to focus on folk dance, creative dance, or modern dance styles such as hip-hop.

New Era, New Rules

While no one denies the American origins of hip-hop, Brazilian b-boys and b-girls would claim it as their own. Beginning in underprivileged neighborhoods, hip-hop grew into a way of life for many young men and women with few academic or employment opportunities. Crews function not only as friends and

> **"**Hip-hop has always been a way to express love, to create art through love. It doesn't have anything to do with the violence and aggression it's often associated with.**"** [4]
>
> —*Marco Olaechea, Bolivian hip-hop producer*

family but also as community service organizations. Many communities have centers that offer workshops in the four pillars of hip-hop: graffiti, dance, rapping, and deejaying. Some nongovernmental organizations have even begun using hip-hop and rap to further literacy campaigns and educate people on public issues such as democracy and sexually transmitted infections.

B-boys and b-girls in Bolivia also use hip-hop as a call for social change. Rappers there hark back to their ancestors, using not only English, Spanish, and Portuguese but also indigenous languages such as Quechua and Aymara. Sdenka Suxo Cadena, a b-girl since the 1990s, helped found a female dance organization in 2000. Men as well as women were welcome to gather, but those who promoted gangs and violence were not permitted to stay.

Even within the United States, hip-hop has been adapted and altered to fit other cultures. While some b-boys and b-girls from Native nations of North America keep their hip-hop selves and Native heritage entirely separate, some have combined parts of both cultures. In fact, aside from the high value placed on rhythm in hip-hop and Native cultures, some Native dance steps can even be seen reflected in hip-hop dance. Mahlikah Awe:ri broke a taboo when she combined drum playing with dancing, but, she argues, hip-hop requires that movement. Hip-hop, with its origins in marginalized communities, can play an important role for Native American and First Nations communities as well. According to John Hupfield, a First Nations MC, hip-hop

Ground Scatter Breakers, a Thai breaking team, dances onstage at the Breakdance World Championship in 2005.

The Japanese team Super Dynamites performs at the 2010 World Hip Hop Dance Championship in Las Vegas, Nevada.

began as a way for African Americans to proudly claim their heritage and to address social issues. This is also how many youth of Native communities use it.

With hip-hop culture in many nations around the world, it probably isn't surprising that there are a number of championship competitions each year. The World Hip Hop Dance Championship is a seven-day annual event, with competitions in breaking, popping, locking, and all styles. The event also includes panel discussions and workshops with prominent dancers and choreographers. Prior to the world championship, each of the nearly 50 affiliated nations, from Uruguay to Ukraine, Canada

to Malaysia, hold national competitions to determine who will represent that country. In conjunction with the World Hip Hop Dance Championship, there are Hip Hop International World Battles—one-on-one competitions in popping, locking, and breaking, and two-on-two competitions in all styles.

Hip-hop isn't just for pros and competitors, though. Even if you don't realize it, you're probably familiar with some of the more popular hip-hop moves. The energy, style, athleticism, and even humor of hip-hop dance are captivating, infectious—and accessible. Anyone can learn to do it.

TIMELINE

1800s

Tap dancing, one of the precursors of hip-hop, develops as a combination of traditional European-American and African-American dances.

1957

The Philadelphia dance and music show *Bandstand* goes national and becomes *American Bandstand*.

1960

Chubby Checker's hit song "The Twist" has everyone across the nation performing a new dance.

1969

Don Campbell develops locking—a whole new style of dance.

1971

Soul Train, a mostly African-American dance and music show, debuts on national television.

1973

DJ Kool Herc pioneers DJ techniques in the Bronx, New York City.

1975

"Boogaloo Sam" Solomon becomes an early developer of popping.

1977

The Rock Steady Crew forms in New York.

1979

The Sugarhill Gang records and releases "Rapper's Delight," which plays on commercial radio and brings rap and hip-hop culture to mainstream audiences.

1983

Of all the television shows and movies featuring hip-hop, *Flashdance* is the first big mainstream hit.

1990–1994

In Living Color, a sketch comedy show created by Keenen Ivory Wayans, features hip-hop dancers called Fly Girls.

2001

The movie *Save the Last Dance* features formal ballet and hip-hop dance.

2002

The first all-hip-hop dance convention, Monsters of Hip-Hop, is held. The annual event hosts classes and brings choreographers and dancers together.

2005

So You Think You Can Dance premieres on television, bringing hip-hop dance to a new generation of viewers.

2008

America's Best Dance Crew premieres on television, sparking renewed interest in hip-hop nationwide.

2015

In January, the groundbreaking rap musical *Hamilton* premieres at the Public Theater (Off-Broadway) in New York.

ESSENTIAL
FACTS

KEY PLAYERS

- Afrika Bambaataa was a DJ from the Bronx. He was one of the originators of hip-hop culture with his breakbeat style of deejaying. Bambaataa and others, such as Grandmaster Flash, followed DJ Kool Herc's example in hosting parties. Together, they helped create and popularize hip-hop culture, which attracted many young people away from gangs.

- James Brown was a legendary singer and performer, known as the "Godfather of Soul". A number of dance moves, and quite a few hip-hop moves in particular, are based on moves Brown originated. His work and music influenced countless other artists and choreographers, including Michael Jackson.

- Don Campbell was a dancer and choreographer best known for inventing locking. The dance spawned a successful dance troupe called the Lockers, which helped spread hip-hop dance throughout the country—and the world—with appearances on *Soul Train* and other mainstream television shows.

- DJ Kool Herc is credited with originating hip-hop music by looping instrumental breaks together, allowing dancers more time to show their moves. He called the dancers break boys and break girls, which became shortened to b-boys and b-girls. He encouraged rapping by allowing MCs to use his microphone during parties.

TRENDS

Hip-hop dance continues to develop and incorporate other forms of dance, music, and art into its orbit. Dancers create new styles and new substyles seemingly every year. However, rather than contracting into one single style, or exploding into unrelated branches of styles, hip-hop dance is likely to continue to encompass many forms of street styles. These styles, developed not in dance studios but by practitioners who are often not formally trained as dancers, will continue to be outlets for marginalized peoples around the world.

LEGACY

Hip-hop dance, which is a vast, sprawling collection of styles and practitioners, is just one pillar of hip-hop culture. This influential culture has been incorporated into nearly every mainstream art form and exists in dozens of countries. Its legacy is its firm establishment, despite its origins as street dance and street culture, and its influence on other art forms, including those not yet developed.

QUOTE

"I think hip-hop has bridged the culture gap. It brings white kids together with black kids, brown kids with yellow kids. They all have something in common that they love. It gets past the stereotypes."

—DJ Kool Herc

GLOSSARY

BREAKING

A style of street dance, also called b-boying or b-girling, and erroneously called break dancing.

CYPHER

In hip-hop, an informal session or competition; also refers to the circle in which b-boys and b-girls dance.

DJ

Disc jockey; the artist who plays the beats and background music in rap songs.

FUNK STYLE

Hip-hop dance style generally developed on the West Coast, such as popping, locking, and boogaloo.

KRUMPING

A style of street dance featuring very energetic, athletic, aggressive movements focused on battles with other dancers.

LOCKING

A style of funk hip-hop dance featuring stop-and-go motion, large movements, tight rhythm, humor, and often very colorful clothing.

MC

A person who speaks over a beat; interchangeable with "rapper."

POPPING

A style of funk hip-hop dance featuring quick stop-and-go motions creating a jerky, animatronic- or robot-like effect.

POWER MOVE

Acrobatic or gymnastic motion used in hip-hop dance, particularly breaking, such as spins, windmills, floats, and flares.

ROBOTING

A dance done with rigid movements to imitate the movement of a robot.

TOPROCK

An element of breaking performed while standing.

TUTTING

A type of popping featuring arm and hand movements of 90 degrees, inspired by ancient Egyptian art.

UPROCKING

An element of hip-hop dance focused on battling with an opponent, though no physical contact is allowed. It uses rhythmic gestures.

WAACKING

A freestyle form of dance emphasizing big but precise arm movements, posing, and physically representing the music.

ADDITIONAL
RESOURCES

SELECTED BIBLIOGRAPHY

Cepeda, Raquel. *And It Don't Stop: The Best American Hip-Hop Journalism of the Last 25 Years*. New York: Faber and Faber, 2004. Print.

Chang, Jeff. *Can't Stop, Won't Stop: A History of the Hip-Hop Generation*. New York: St. Martin's, 2005. Print.

Fricke, Jim, and Charlie Ahearn. *Yes Yes Y'all: The Experience Music Project Oral History of Hip-Hop's First Decade*. Cambridge, MA: Da Capo, 2002. Print.

Fuhrer, Margaret. *American Dance: The Complete Illustrated History*. Minneapolis: Voyageur, 2014. Print.

Ogbar, Jeffrey O. G. *Hip-Hop Revolution: The Culture and Politics of Rap*. Lawrence: U of Kansas, 2007. Print.

FURTHER READINGS

Bailey, Diane. *A History of Dance*. Minneapolis: Abdo, 2015. Print.

Cummings, Judy Dodge. *Hip-Hop Culture*. Minneapolis: Abdo, 2017. Print.

WEBSITES

To learn more about Hip-Hop Insider, visit **abdobooklinks.com**. These links are routinely monitored and updated to provide the most current information available.

FOR MORE INFORMATION

For more information on this subject, contact or visit the following organizations:

CULTURE SHOCK INTERNATIONAL
2110 Hancock Street, Suite 200
San Diego, CA 92110
619-299-2110
http://www.cultureshockdancecenter.com/
This network of nonprofit dance companies in the United States and Canada is working to educate students of all ages and build communities through hip-hop dance.

EVERYBODY DANCE NOW!
1460 Broadway, 17th floor
New York, NY 10036
347-354-3536
http://www.everybodydancenow.org/
This nonprofit organization encourages healthy, active lifestyles, respect for self and others, and friendship through hip-hop dance.

HIP HOP INTERNATIONAL
8033 Sunset Boulevard, #920
Los Angeles, California 90046
323-850-3777
http://www.hiphopinternational.com
Hip Hop International showcases information about national and international competitions, qualifying competitions, and workshops.

SOURCE NOTES

CHAPTER 1. HIP-HOP MAKES HISTORY

1. "The Rockefeller Foundation Announces $6 Million in Additional Funding for 100,000 Inner City Students Nationwide to see *Hamilton*." *News & Media*. The Rockefeller Foundation, 23 June 2016. Web. 24 Oct. 2016.

2. Lisa Robinson. "Questlove and Lin-Manuel Miranda Give Details of *The Hamilton Mixtape*." *Vanity Fair*. Vanity Fair, Mar. 2016. Web. 17 Oct. 2016.

3. Suraya Mohamed. "'Hamilton': A Story of Us." *NPR Music*. NPR, 20 June 2016. Web. 21 Oct. 2016.

4. Suzannah Friscia. "Hamilton's Dance Revolution." *Dance Magazine*. DanceMedia LLC, 31 May 2016. Web. 19 Oct. 2016.

CHAPTER 2. HIP-HOP DANCE ORIGINS

None.

CHAPTER 3. LOCKING AND POPPING

1. Wendy Garofoli. "Urban Legend." *Dance Spirit*. 1 Apr. 2008. *HighBeam Research*. Web. 21 Oct. 2016.

2. Jeff Chang. *Total Chaos: The Art and Aesthetics of Hip-Hop*. New York: Civitas Books, 2007. Print. 22.

3. Wendy Garofoli. "Urban Legend." *Dance Spirit*. 1 Apr. 2008. *HighBeam Research*. Web. 21 Oct. 2016.

4. "Soul Train." *TV Series Finale*. TV Series Finale, n.d. Web. 15 Oct. 2016.

5. Jeff Chang. *Total Chaos: The Art and Aesthetics of Hip-Hop*. New York: Civitas Books, 2007. Print. 23.

6. Wendy Garofoli. "Urban Legend." *Dance Spirit*. 1 Apr. 2008. *HighBeam Research*. Web. 21 Oct. 2016.

7. Brian Seibert. "Breaking Down." *Village Voice*. Village Voice, 26 Oct. 2004. Web. 13 Oct. 2016.

SOURCE NOTES
CONTINUED

CHAPTER 4. BREAKING IN THE BRONX

1. Michael Eric Dyson. *Know What I Mean? Reflections on Hip-Hop.* New York: Civitas Books, 2007. Print. 75.

2. "Hip-Hop vs. Rap." *Genius.* Genius Media Group, n.d. Web. 15 Oct. 2016.

CHAPTER 5. DANCE CREWS AND BATTLES

1. Jeff Chang. *Can't Stop Won't Stop: A History of the Hip-Hop Generation.* New York: St. Martin's, 2007. Print. xi.

CHAPTER 6. FAD AND PARTY DANCES

None.

CHAPTER 7. NEW SCHOOL

1. Alan J. Klopman. "Interview with Popin' Pete & Mr. Wiggles, Monsters of Hip-Hop." *Dance.com*. Dance.com, Jan. 2007. Web. 15 Oct. 2016.

2. Anna Gaca. "New York Public Library to Acquire Archive of Hip-hop Dance." 30 Sept. 2016. *SPIN*. Spin, Web. 16 Oct. 2016.

CHAPTER 8. AROUND THE WORLD

1. "Hip-Hop from Germany at the Dance World Cup in Las Vegas." *Deutschland*. Frankfurter Societäts-Medien, 6 Aug. 2013. Web. 17 Oct. 2016.

2. Eriko Arita. "Street Dance Sweeps Young Japan."*Japan Times*. Japan Times, 23 Sept. 2012. Web. 17 Nov. 2016.

3. Renuka Rayasam. "Germany's Young Muslims Are Turning to Hip-Hop to Express Their Feelings." *Quartz*. Quartz, 1 Feb. 2016. Web. 2 Nov. 2016.

4. Andrew Cummings. "The Experimental Side of Hip-Hop." *Bolivian Express Magazine*. Bolivian Express Magazine, 22 Oct. 2010. Web. 16 Nov. 2016.

INDEX

ABOUT THE AUTHORS

Audrey DeAngelis studied anthropology and history at James Madison University. She works as a historical interpreter at an eighteenth-century museum and is a firm believer that the past affects us every day.

Gina DeAngelis has written dozens of books and articles for young people (and older ones) on a wide variety of subjects. She loves learning new things and is not particularly fly.